LOUDER BIRDS

LOUDER BIRDS

ANGELA VORAS-HILLS

PLEIADES
PRESS

THE LENA-MILES WEVER TODD POETRY SERIES
Warrensburg, MO

Library of Congress Control Number:
978-0-8071-7299-5

Published by Pleiades Press

Department of English
University of Central Missouri
Warrensburg, Missouri 64093

Distributed by Louisiana State University Press

Cover Image: Katie Musolff, "Amen"
Author Photo: Matthew Hills
Cover design by Sarah Nguyen
Book design by David Wojciechowski

First Pleiades Printing, 2020

Financial support for this project has been provided by the University of
Central Missouri and the Missouri Arts Council, a state agency.

for Matthew & Carter

CONTENTS

RETROSPECTIVE

A girl stands barefoot beside a wheelbarrow,
shoulders bare, holding a plywood sign that reads:

> Zucchini
> and God

in red paint. Her hair snarls in the wind
and rain, but she doesn't notice. Like any sign,

it's difficult to know how seriously to take it.
The sky is gray. A cat darts from the field

of corn, and crosses the street, disappearing
into the forest. Clouds drop from the sky

and cover the grass, the fields, the trees.
The boundaries between home and the road

are insecure: it's impossible to navigate this landscape.
We've all been in the presence of something dark

and have chosen not to seek shelter. There are sirens.
There will be sirens. Looking back, it's clear—

the girl has disappeared. For now, the puddle remains
unnamed, so it is not yet a disaster.

ON MY WAY HOME

A great horned owl sits in the window
of a silo along the highway. The foundation

of the barn is now rubble, its boards salvaged.
My mother has scraped and painted the wood

into plant stands. On the other side
of the highway, flames chew clean

to the steel skeleton of a sedan, its body
barely identifiable. Firemen stand close

with the hose, but no water comes through.
There's no ambulance. The lake

has recently frozen over. Yesterday,
firemen gathered on it, jumped hard

to collapse the shell and fell through.
Each body tall in a black dry-suit, then,

only a watery hole where they'd stood.
The mother of one of the men watched

in the snow beside me. Just then,
my son was in biology class.

But what he was learning about the body,
I don't know.

AT THE PERIPHERY, WHERE LIFE HUMS

A white box is not the house, the house
is not white. The house cannot be separated
from the white barn, which is also not white,
because the wood is rotting, and its silo
is silver. The beige Formica table
on its chrome legs cannot be removed
from the kitchen. There are always
Oatmeal Cream Pies in the cupboard.
But the children can leave, and have left,
and she remains with her mind separating
into blue and red. Now, someone must be paid
to remove the pins from her gray hair
and tie her shoes. There is an illusion of life
when the colors connect: the doll she carries
in her arms is the memory of all her children.
She hums to them. She still hums, though they
have grown and gone, and she cries, and in the corner,
Mary is mourning, and the Bible is always
open to a page. She may know the words by heart.
She may not understand them at all. Today, the pages
are blank. The Bible cannot be removed from the house.
The house is not white, the garden is not green, the apples
hang heavy and will soon collapse, covering the ground.

PRESERVING

I can spend a whole winter
      in the summer of these lemons
            if they're covered in enough salt.

            Trucks are salting the roads
      so I can drive. Men
salt the earth so I can walk

without falling. When I fall,
      I catch myself with my face.
            When I fall, I go

            to the hospital, to make sure
      the baby is still alive.
There are so many small things

to worry about in a large way.
      How much coffee should I drink?
            For every bean ground, someone

            is having sex or a child
      is starving. How do I know?
Because I'm always reading

warning labels or watching
      children pick dandelions near the slide.
            Except they are never

dandelions, but toads. And the children
      pick them up and throw them
            into the pond by the handful,

believing they are frogs.
And we can't blame them for not knowing
what swims, what sinks, what floats.

CONTROLLED BURN

The doe ran into the road, flipped
over our hood and dragged her back legs

across the highway into woods. The same day,
they were killing a man in Oklahoma

who wouldn't die, they were deciding
when to try again, and men in masks

and bright orange suits set fire to the marsh—
the burning flesh of milkweed and switchgrass.

We are told to be fruitful. We are told
to rejoice. The next day, a hospital bed

is set up in the front room of the farmhouse
whose roof might collapse at any minute. As though

the heavens are aware of the weight
of a minute, as though each minute

responds solely to the sky. It's illegal
to follow an injured deer

into woods with a gun,
but is it ok to tell a child about heaven

if you don't believe it exists? *Yes,*
sing the chorus frogs,

who'd burrowed into the heart
of the marsh to escape the flames.

No, hisses the body
of a vole squashed flat,

perfectly filling
a crack in the blacktop.

NOTHING TO UNDO THAT CAN'T
BE DONE AGAIN

On the first day, we ripped carpet from the room's bones,
rolled it like clay, stacked ourselves into man, and ate

eggs Benedict in the breakfast nook. Light fell like a body
through the ceiling, onto our plates, and we ate.

      Our neighbors were sleeping in our walls,
      we could hear them across fields. We tore the paper down,

      found we were equal parts inside and out. As though
      we were the windows our neighbors looked into at night.

As though our brights were on and no one would flash
to warn us. On the third day, we laid our hammers

on maps of places we'd been, tacked photos
onto our cupboards. We'd forgotten plates and forks,

      took seriously what fruit flies confirmed about memory
      and sleep. We couldn't trust the water slapping the shore downhill

      from a sea of corn. The oak fence was barbed in the backyard:
      when it fell, nobody called to tell us. Eagle, coyote, turkey—

on the eighth day, the farmer shot them all and loosened
the sheep's noose. His collie chased everything to pasture.

WHEN ALL AROUND US SKY AND
ONE PERPETUAL FLAME

Then we must allow for answers in clouds, their shadows
covering half the prairie. Or crows, swooping in and out
of sunlight, searching for a perch. Yes, we could leave this place
for another—build again by sea, let salt lick our lips, rub
our eyes raw—but we'd miss the sweet nesting of storks
on the phone-pole beside the landfill. How silent our lives
without the hammering clatter of their bills before sunrise,
the smell of loss rotting behind our house. Watching them
land, pick through chicken heads, sausages, fish skins,
their ballet of wing splay and turn, the gentle tug of their bills
as they pull apart, lift their necks, and swallow. The delicate
flight back to brood, disgorging of food, the nestlings
eager to eat. Why should they leave this place? Already
winter's unfurling, its clouds shrinking from the sun, the sky
just as everywhere as always. Listen to all the air we can hold
when we prop these hand-drawn walls in place with our breath.

IN WHICH I HOARD THE AIR ESCAPING

An abundance of crows—cats pick their meat,
scatter beaks and legs between bushes,

and bring the black wings back to the field.

We hold hands through wheat, scapulae snapping
beneath us, and lay our blanket at the shorn edge

to watch the murder convene in branches.

Grasshoppers, hayflies, golden
breeze—you speak of love as a flame

tickling the skin of our house. So I gather

your breath like photographs and salt,
blankets and hoses, hoping

the neighbor's dog will sniff us out

before our walls collapse. The sun sinks, and the crows
disappear in the darkness. I'd begun to mistake them

for promises. *It's impossible to know*, you say,

as the cat climbs on my lap to watch
the field of crows picking at bones between us.

HAPPENED TO FIND THE BARN EMPTY

Thought yellow about corn
still green, grass still yellow,

and the coop wall collapsed
facing east. Sun kept the eggs.

Not you. In the garden, morning
glories. In the center, a cement

calf painted Holstein, its gray nose
crumbling. Your hands lit

leaves in the backyard.
The cat stretched in the ditch,

whiskered the mouse
toward no small burning.

UNFURLING

After the seasonal fires filled our lungs,
we washed the linens. The neighbor's cat lingered
      on our windowsill, looking in. We couldn't

get rid of him, no matter the poison. By that time,
      we'd known for months. The grass
had been singed by soil, worms

      lay shriveled in dirt. We waited
all night near the window for crickets, didn't hear
      the opossum digging its way in

through the foundation of our house.
      It curled into a ball behind the dryer to die.
Days later, the sidewalk was glistening black,

      covered with the crickets' silent bodies.
You carried me to the car and began
      driving. When the urge came

to push, I hesitated, but couldn't resist
      the burning. The moon sat quietly above
the ribs of the earth. Somewhere, tides were rising.

ON THE EVE OF THE DEATH OF THE PATRON SAINT OF THOSE WHOSE LIVES ARE LOST TO SOMETHING SCIENCE CAN'T EXPLAIN

Never mind the robin's red breast, legs twitching upright in the road,
the sparrow on the curb, his head twisted backwards, or all the blackbirds
falling from the sky at once. The crows have taken the last
bit of bread to the puddle: let them call to warn the others.
We'll open the windows so the remaining birds can gather
at the foot of her bed. Let her rest here until they come.

MUSS ES SEIN? ES MUSS SEIN!

—after John Wilde

Because the moon is a wafer
         bleeding beneath my tongue,
                and the desert is still sleeping,
        it must be. Tomorrow

stands with its toes at the edge
          of a volcano, pouring
                a red mess of life
        from its stomach

into the earth's pit.
         If the day's not picked apart
                first by the bills
        of louder birds,

I will tear into it like bread.
         This is how the rhythm
                of the earth's core will continue
        beating. Yes, it must

be this light in my hair or
         the moon's muted halo
                through which the stars swim
        like minnows

in a bait shop tub. It must be
         the weight of my face
                in my hands or
        the weight of the body

hanging from the meat hook,
      watching with hollow eyes,
          waiting for a slip
    of the blade to release it.

ON EARTH AS IT IS IN HEAVEN

Days after my mom finishes radiation, she's in Vegas
on a Harley. It's 80 degrees, and she sends selfies
with cocktails in the sun. Here, everything is beginning
to thaw: the body of ice thunders and pings and cracks
in its undoing. When I was young, I believed the lake
froze through completely, along with the creatures
inside: glass-eyed fish, bug-eyed frogs, painted turtles
with wrinkled legs and necks stuck outstretched.
But then the lake was pocked with shanties, and men
in orange hats and snowsuits hoisted northern pike
up through icy holes—their shiny bodies struggling
as they were pulled by their lips into sky. The idea
of heaven is ridiculous and comforting
and full of misdirection. In that same winter
of my childhood, my grandpa landed his plane
on the lake. A few days later, his friend learned
he had brain cancer and shot himself. The funeral home
was covered in yellow lilies, white roses, but his wife
was not relieved. In the basement of the church,
we ate ham and potato casserole and prayed
holding hands. All year long, we filled our freezer
with fish, sun warming us at the kitchen sink
as my mother slipped her knife into their bodies—
peeling away their skin, slicing their flesh into pieces.

BAKE SALES

We brought guns to the firehouse bake sale,
shot into the eroded hill, bought carrot cake

with cream cheese frosting. Snow
forced everything from the walls.

We caught the carpet-mouse, left him
asleep in a box with crayoned windows.

At church, the priest must've said something
before we sang *Hallelujah*. Our hands

must've been cold, even in mittens.
Climbing into the truck, frost snagged

our tights and dresses, our bodies smashed
together on vinyl seats for warmth.

We raced to the front porch to lick
the icicle hanging from gutter to ground, found

Amy laughing in the doorway wearing jeans,
her purple socks sinking in the burnt orange

shag with olive freckles. Amy is always
in the doorway laughing. In the front yard snow

the mouse's blood is always red.
We waited inside until sunshine, grass, then ice

melted in our lemonade cooler. Some men
gave us five dollars for a Dixie cup full

and drove away waving, their lips wet.

CAMOUFLAGE

The more I writhe to detangle my body
      from the net the poachers set at the edge
         of the forest, the deeper the leaves

      of your vest blend in with the bark
of the tree I dangle from.
      Below, a mirror reflects the sun

which makes me want to live
      through your scent like summer.
         I need to make like a puddle

      and collect myself: Once,
I was a child. My neighbor had a pool
      in her backyard. Her dad collected matchbooks

with naked women on the inside.
      Sometimes I would steal them.
         This has so little to do with you, except

sometimes, I can't help myself.
      And this is why I need you
         to carry a knife, and why I want you

to let me fall
and break all of my earthly bones.

PERSONA

Before I had language, I laughed: How many men does it take
to build a house? How many women are left to make the beds?

I played on a crooked bridge, walked the planks until the suspension
gave, and rusted bolts caught my skin. I ran home, bleeding.

Before I owned cliché, I pushed my baby in a stroller and tucked her
into her crib. I was five and licking the beaters of someone else's

cake batter. I picked each cherry from the pie and left its shell
untouched. This is how I learned to want everyone

to want to understand me. By the time I was old enough
to dissect meaning from the body, the windows

had been sealed shut. I began separating
yolks from their whites, seeds from their hulls, and now

I can finally taste leaves loosening from their branches.
I roll in the dirt that will catch them.

PAINTING THE GARAGE

The only thing I'd imagined bigger was the backyard.
And missing: pheasants across the street, the brush,

too, and the willow, which we may have dug up
ourselves before leaving. Brown tractor tire?

Still around the maple's base. The new mom
and three daughters sat on the back-door stoop.

I dipped my brush in a bucket of glue,
pulled the bristles across their lips.

They sat at the kitchen table as I opened
their fridge, stuck my finger into a jar of frosting,

tore into their cake. After she ate, the mother
followed me to the garage with laundry on her hip.

Through my bedroom window, the girls
gawked with dark eyes at falling leaves.

Beneath the garage's walls were the brick and mortar
I remembered. I painted each brick white, watched it dry

as the mother set the porch swing on the picnic table,
letting her feet dangle. When the paint set, I peeled

tape from the panes through which I'd once watched
the leaves fall and took off down Miami Circle on my bike.

ALWAYS THE LAST PLACE YOU LOOK

There was no last train waiting
          at the platform. I walked
with my ears plugged to a bar

          and drank rail rum and RC Cola.
The cigarette machines hummed—
          there was no jukebox.

I'd have played "Get Out of My Dreams."
          The pool table was filled
with cue balls. Where I grew up, the pool

          had a water slide, but before that,
it was a dirt hole filled with water.
          It was surrounded by chain-link,

so we paid to get in.
          Of course, there was a slide
in the mud hole, too, but it was metal

          and burned. Then, they lined
the hole with cement and filled it. I failed
          three rounds of swimming lessons

before my brother
          pushed me into the deep end.
Each Thanksgiving, I say

          thank you, and we eat
green bean casserole, turkey,
          and squash.

DEAR ABBY,

I won't tell anyone you prefer nachos to sex—
there's limited ammo for breeze-shooting,
        but I won't use yours. I try
        to avoid guns, though my father keeps
            an oak cabinet full of rifles. He's never
            boarded a plane, but once told security
my mom had a bomb in her purse.
(This was before psychics felt tremors
        in their palms.) Last night, I spent
        twenty minutes listening to hold music
            on speaker phone, eating oranges
            over the kitchen sink. My tea leaves
unfurled, said "stay," so I curled
fetal into bed, an African goat-
        bludgeoning club on my nightstand,
        and dreamt of a baby who could swim
            to shore in a riptide. I woke up,
            taped price tags to all my furniture,
and hauled it onto the lawn. It began raining
before anyone could take it away.

ANOTHER POEM NOT ABOUT A BABY

It should've stayed a dream,
but we'd rearranged the living room,

tore down the wall, lengthening the space,

added a big screen at one end
—all your idea. The neighbor knocked.

He wanted to come in from the rain

for a craft brew and football. We barely
knew him, but he sat on our couch, propped

his feet on our table. I sat on the floor

cocooned in a quilt, eyes closed
as you grabbed a book to smash

the centipede skittering across the wall,

seeking a crack in our plaster.
A few nights earlier, we'd watched the spider

spindle from the ceiling to the rug.

And where was the cat?
He'd become suspicious of my lap,

kneading it too long before settling in.

I'd been on the couch for days,
swallowed too much without chewing.

There was nothing I could wash down and keep.

HOME (IV)

On the other side of the field, the old house
was still asleep. When the father disappeared,
nobody was around to answer questions.
For a year, we watched what grew and died
between our house and theirs. Among all the mothers
in the field, only the coyote had eaten her young.
When the chamomile finally bloomed, we wore
tall boots and trampled her rotten den.
Through the shattered kitchen window, we saw
blood, black beneath the table where
no light could touch it. We crawled in
to be closer. Touching the blood made us
invisible to the birds, and the sun
could not reach us. Pots and pans were still
on the stove, the toaster beside a sink
full of black dishes. We held hands
and curled into the corner of a dark room.
We waited for some small light to find us.

AND STILL WITH LIGHT IN YOUR EYES

Two foxes run circles
            around the cement wall
                        of a reflecting pool.

Someone has unnamed them.

I point them out to you,
            and they stop
                        to consider us

through the glass. We're just

sitting down to breakfast.
            You pour salt
                        into piles on the table,

toss pinches over your shoulders.

I should know better
            than to speak, but I call them
                        Conclusion and Prudence.

The renaming casts shadows

on their bodies. Our plates are full.
            A basket of pears rots on the back
                        porch. There are no animals

left to be seen, but the scent

of fur lingers around the cement
            pool, and the pool
                        remains empty.

NEVER A GOOD TIME

We'd been up all night
in separate rooms
when the baby first fluttered.

I stared into darkness until
sunlight clung to fog above the trees.
This morning, snow

is finally falling. The goat,
ankle-deep in water, has lost
his tail-hair to mites. Pickets

of our fence collect downstream
with remnants of the coop.
Months ago, you filled jars

with fluids, folded the chickens'
naked wings into them, and lined
the walls of our root cellar.

The rest of the jars are empty.
When our walls collapse,
we'll expect answers

to questions we haven't asked.

GROWING SEASON

On the bike path, a bunny's body and blood
where the head should be. Something

has torn off its foot, something has eaten
its heart, its entrails frozen in snow.

The plow growls past me. This morning
I left eggs behind the couch to incubate. I spent

last night walking until all the blood left my feet,
and my thighs throbbed. The snow

refuses to melt. I refuse to wear
a sweater set or heels. Instead of TV news,

I watch the sky. When it darkens,
my ribs swell, and I know it is not time

to plant. I wait for the beginning
or the end—depending on the day. Soon,

there will be enough water for all of us
to need to build a boat: the sun falls

into the street, blinding the drivers heading
north, warming the snow from inside.

NEVER EAT A POLAR BEAR'S LIVER

The crocuses' purple mouths,
finally opened to the sun,

      fill with snow. Their necks
      snap under the weight, heads
      hang heavy toward the ground.

If I could go longer without
showering, if I could buy

      more in bulk, sit still, stop
      driving, eat less. The BBC
      says a teaspoon of polar bear

liver contains enough vitamin A
to kill, which, if you're lost

      with sled dogs in the arctic
      is good to know, but really,
      how much longer will it matter?

The polar bear is lumbering
toward its Latin root:

      maritimus: of the sea, inconstant.
      As though a holdover from the ark,
      it's born with paws partially

webbed, covered in papillae,
given a name unstable as ice…

I admit, I can't help looking
both ways before crossing
a one-way street. As a kid,

I collected cans in bags, hauled them
to the Golden Goat for change.

How am I still stubborn enough
to believe in some small reward
for my hand-washed yogurt cups

picked up curbside on Mondays?
I find hope in tending

red worms digesting scraps in a bin
beneath my sink. I keep the paper
shreds fresh—last week's news

billowing above the worms
like cumulous clouds:

Tsunami in Japan. New
drug for Parkinson's. Today's
forecast: sunny, a high of 72.

REFLEX

Fumble on the big screen, everyone
up in arms. My daughter grasps my shirt
          while nursing and can't let go. Across the room,
          my mother applies Chapstick without taking
her eyes off the screen. It's Christmas. Everyone believes
in miracles and wants to hold the baby. My grandmother
          sits at the table holding a doll. Beyond her, a train
          slips through the snowy field carrying—what? Time
moves backwards on the field. Less than a minute left
on the clock. My grandmother's lips barely close around the red
          spoonful of Jell-O with coconut. A marshmallow falls
from the spoon in all its puffed-up,
childhood ecstasy. The game is nearly over. Pins
          and needles. The tree is heavy with color
          and ornaments of beans and children's faces.
My grandmother tightens her fingers around the hanky
she has always held. Eventually, there is nothing
          left beneath the tree. Everyone kisses the baby.
          They each slip a finger into her palm,
and she struggles to let them go.

SELF-PORTRAIT AS A CAT TRAPPED IN A MOTEL ROOM

However many more lives I have,

I'll fall hard to this earth
        and bruise easily. I'm glad

        I didn't know not to dip my toes
into the lake's shallows for fear

of leeches. True, I held the sea

deep in my chest and nearly drowned
        in the salt of its longing, but

        I'd have been swallowed gladly
by the tide. Someone warned me not to jar fireflies

in my mouth, but I welcomed the attraction

of moths to their light, loved walking
        in the powder of their white wings

        on the wooden floor. But now,
windows bolted, I want to forget

the pleasures of pacing a ledge, the smell

of cardinals and trees and sky.
        I've torn apart the black-out drapes

        to give my body to the sun. I refuse
to leave anything beneath the bed—

everything I dragged in, I'll take out with me.

AS IF THE SUN

I'm in love with the middle-aged couple
kissing in the driveway before work. Her hand around
a travel mug, two teenage boys waiting in the backseat
of a silver four-door. A woman approaches them barefoot
with a broom, a bandana covering her hair. She's not
sweeping, but singing, wandering into the road
beside a line of parked cars to avoid the couple.

As if the sun has realized April might come
to an end, it's trying to shine through the wind.
Longing twitters from the small, red body of a cardinal
beside a nest in the forsythia. I consider the grass, the heat
on my bare face, the weight of the cup in my hand.
And in that moment: a crow, a hawk, a starling.

THE SPIDER

—after Jane Hirshfield

The spider was yellow, iridescent, large, and equally
alarmed. Skittering from an old stack of coupons,
to the darkness behind the counter, as nature instructed.

As I, at times, have pulled the blankets over my face
when the floorboards creaked, closed my eyes as if
there were not a child sleeping in the next room.

And now, another mother in the kitchen, I bleach
the countertop where the spider's cotton sac
exploded, scattering her eggs like crystals of sugar.

A DRAIN FULL OF EELS

The sewer grate was covered in eels, but who knew
where they came from? Not the guy tossing tackle in the bed
of his pickup. Their mouths were bleeding and flies
had begun a sunny afternoon feast. The smell of their bellies
rose like heat from a charcoal grill, and, in their eyes,

Barbara, a stranger with dirty blonde hair and yellow
peep-toe wedges. She'd asked me to read poems out loud
on a bus crowded with after-workers in suits and flip flops.
As we reached her stop, she picked a scab off her leg,
exhaled: *God's making me more visible every day.*

APPEARING CLOSER

From the highway, the face of a woman echoed orange in the window
        of a house equally echoing orange. There was a face,

                and then there were shadows. I swerved from the shadows,
                as if from deer, though knowing better

        is to brake. I never thought
to brake. As when, in another time, you'd told me

not to break, so I didn't. Once, I knew a woman who swerved from a deer
            and hit a pole and woke up to learn her eight-year-old daughter
            had died, and yet I didn't

break. And then another night, because the calendar had been missing
            from the fridge for days, and we'd forgotten

to keep track of time, I wound up naked in the front yard.
        You emptied your paper bag and told me to cover up and wait.
            I sat on the lawn,
                letting the moon smooth over me,

                      despite your fear of its falling.
      And then, another time, I told you to hold me
        like I was ice cream.
            That day, it was in the 80s, and we kept

the car windows rolled up as though we were dogs, and we wanted
        to prove we wanted to live. I made you promise
            to keep them closed,
        even as I began to melt.

FOR PITY'S SAKE, SPEAK TO ME

You thought I was the kind of girl who'd sink
          to the bottom of a well for an opal
while you flew to the shores of another
          woman's mouth. Over each glass
of port, the bells chimed. You left oysters
          rotting in your bucket while standing
knee-deep in the river, sifting its floor for gold.
          Meanwhile, I found your name scratched
 into the door of an outhouse, around which
          ermines began to gather. I slit the skin
from their bodies to warm my neck, you tore
          a page out of the phone book before slipping
your hand into my pants. We kept warm
          this way for years, locking each other
in phone booths, watching as others knocked
          on our glass walls, hoping to reach us.

A SMALL HOLE FILLED WITH MUD

I'm at the salt lick in the backyard
of the man who placed it there.

I've found the pile of apples
in the clearing of the forest.

The trees, their needles and leaves,
are breathless. Not even a cloud

blinks. I woke in an empty field
after spending my last night with you

on a sticky wooden dance floor.
I'm still not sure which hat

you're hiding under. I am waiting
for the man to see me through

the screen door. I've left bouquets
of dandelions wilting in the swamp.

Children who won't exist are calling
my name: we'd given each a name.

I am up to my ankles and sinking,
taking the last of the sun down with me.

YOUNG PEOPLE IN LOVE ARE
NEVER HUNGRY

Night thick as molasses, grizzlies dance
for the man with a girl's face

in his lap: they'll do anything
for a quick meal. Though the pond

behind has gone to muck, lily pads still expose
their shiny bellies in a breeze, turn up

frogs, all asleep. Like dormant creatures,
the girl's breasts are inked full

of starlings in another woman's nest,
a mess of bills, feathers, legs knocking

out the eggs, the eggs falling
like hair clumped from a brush.

Starlings flee feeders when darkness
crowds the fields, unlike bears,

who sleep until the lamps shine
on dumpsters. Then they follow

the scent of something sweet
or dome-light-dead as a parked car.

Under the moon, where fifteen minutes
is too long to idle, the bear lies alone

on its back. It bites into many fruits
before it finds the black plum
is sweetest when it gives
to light pressure between its paws.

ABANDONED NEST

There were enough leaves around my feet
       to bury a child.

          A second moon had been predicted,

      but looking up through branches,
I saw only bones

      pricking through the floor of a nest—

        their existence a sign
            of nothing. When you left,

I searched your half-empty drawers, discovered

      you were erratic as the sky.
        Still, I wrapped my neck in your barbs

      of pearl and lace, climbed the fort's ladder

to hold it down alone. I was barefoot.
      The walls were eggshell.

        Bottles of shampoo stiffened on the tub's rim,

      lawn chairs rusted in gravel.
The boys had left

      guns in the closets. They would be back

        soon for sandwiches. In the living room,
      the buck's head collected dust.
I waited, washing dishes in water I couldn't see through

until only air sputtered from the faucet, cold
   as a memory of your voice or wind

creaking in the boughs and then

the first snow falls. All winter, mice take solace
  in the woodshed, eat the poison.

    The boys stop to eat and leave.

  Through the kitchen window,
I watch the owl collapse

  like a white log from the oak branch.

    I empty the fridge of pickles and ketchup
 long expired

and leave the door open for the light—

WAIT IN THE BATHTUB AND IT WILL CARRY YOU

In the basement, the puddle of ants needed
           to be dealt with. We built them a bridge
then warmed our mugs of water
           in the attic to avoid the flood. Too many
days went by without our caring
           for the tulips. When we remembered
to expose them to light, it was fall
           and the chestnuts had already popped
free from their pods. We were never
           the type to plant on time,
relied on chipmunks to eat
           the tomatoes and excrete their seeds
in convenient patterns within
           a square of chicken wire. Our rose bushes
rose from the side of our house,
           and grew toward whatever
they could believe in. We, on the other hand,
           laid in the grass like two oceans
beneath a full moon, one of us
           always waxing or waning and waiting
for someone else to build a pier
           onto which we might tie our small ship.

ALL-INCLUSIVE TRIP TO THE LAND
OF MILK AND HONEY

Wombats were sleeping in my womb. We were waiting
for better air, the moment

the mongoose might loosen
its tongue from my mouth. My panties were bunched

in the corner of the room. A man carried a rabbit
by its hindlegs through the thicket

of my forehead. It was bleeding. You couldn't see
the man or the rabbit, but you could see

the blood. My eyes had sunk
to the bottom of the hope chest. They were better

left there, dilated and underexposed. You'd been,
just the other day, to the nude beach.

All of that flesh and nothing but skin to protect it.

ENCOURAGE BIRDS

I tuck my head into my lap.
              Old songs play
        between the warnings.
I light a candle and watch
              centipedes skitter
        up the walls. In the end,
it was worth it
              to have imagined stars
        dancing near the sump pump.

Bees who'd shimmied
              through mortar fissures
        to escape winter were unable
to squeeze back through
and lay dead
        in circles on the cement floor.

To catch earwigs,
              create a dark space
        for them to crawl into
or encourage birds.
              The basement is full
        of boxes with pinholes. Upstairs,

the cat has scattered
              imprints of his nose
        along the window, inches
from where the feeder swayed.
He meows,
        but I can't hear him
among the collapse
              and shatter. Still,
        I believe he's there.

CONFESSIONAL

I come from a long line of men
who cut holes in their boxer shorts.

If I haven't shown up somewhere
naked, I haven't shown up

alone. When I was twelve, I sat
in the bushes in front of my house, luring

boys to my lawn with carrots. After the rain,
I pulled a sewer grate up from the road

to rescue a bunny who'd hopped in.
There are plenty of dirty things you can do

in the sewer. Sex shouldn't be one of them.
You'd expect to see rats in the sewer,

but I was 26 before I saw a rat in real life.
It was on my patio, eating sunflower seeds

that had fallen from the birdfeeder.
I brought it in and fed it grapes. I let it crawl

through my fleece blanket and sit
on my shoulder like a parrot. I washed

my hands thoroughly. I washed my body
in the shower and let my husband

scrub my back with a loofah.
Sometimes I ask him to braid my hair.

KRAKOW

I left two children and a cat
sitting alone on a plane.
       It was coach, I refused
       the in-flight chicken.

Once my feet touched ground,
my scarf smelled like blood.
       I was probably dying
       of something nobody'd heard of.

A butcher offered lemon
soup with fresh sprigs
       I couldn't identify, but ate
       nonetheless. It was impossible

to get a comb through my hair
without a German Shepherd
       sniffing me out in the courtyard.
       I must've been quite alive:

I drank seltzer to calm
my nerves, wound myself down
       into salt mines. After shots
       of tequila in an orange, vinyl pub,

its walls of stone and earth,
I escaped the clutches of a trench-
       coated man pissing in a brick
       corner. All my mittens

soggy in the rain. I dried them
in creperies, fell in love
　　　　with the touch of pigeons
　　　　roosting in my coat and hair.

MAPS OF PLACES DRAWN TO SCALE

Ten minutes from a two-week vacation,
  a van flips on an exit ramp. In a small town,
   the van is bigger. On the highway,
  it's just a van, heading toward a hotel. This
is global positioning: a man is ejected and the van
  lands on top of him. In a small town, a priest
   knows the man's name, but Death does not
  concern itself with formalities. It also does not take
the man whole: only his legs and anything else
  it can grab below the waist. At a Chinese buffet,
   Death is stuffing her cheeks
  with crab rangoons, while a family
stands behind her with empty plates. Nobody stuck
  to the vinyl booth finds "You will suffer"
   inside their cookie, but it's implied
  in the parking lot. A child breaks free
from her mother's arms and runs head-first
  into traffic. In the city, there are always
   detours. But in a small town, there's one
  name for each baby born, and eventually
it's on the lips of everyone in the street.

RABBIT IN THE ROAD

Blood spooling away from its head,
the threads collecting in a pool
on the center line. There was nowhere
we could look without seeing it. It continued
spilling out like oil, and I began to regret
walking —your little hand holding
a dish of blue moon, my heavy cone
of rocky road. It had grown dark. I pointed up
at the Bear, but we were barefoot and couldn't ignore
the blood rising over the curb, onto the sidewalk:
it was slick between our toes, sticking
to the arches of our feet—we had to watch
our step. Ahead of us lay a path
of infinite bridges. We crossed one
after the other, following red tracks
left to dry and finally found our house:
the door left open, hallway walls covered
in the blue light of the moon.

A TRIBUTE TO FEBRUARY

—after John Wilde

Ribbon bleeding from a tree,
the tree a zebra, the sand
beneath its hooves repeating
strands of mauve, pink, gray.
But no hooves, only red heels
filled with white feet, white calves,
legs quitting at the knee, knees
filled with prairie flowers
grown wild in some man's
pants. By now, we know the zebra
is nothing. Already, February
has taken us like sugar, it beats
in our blood like a woman released
from gravity. If the woman
lets go of her rose, if she falls
from the stippled moon-dust sky.
If February is the moon, it's all
there is if we survive. No need
for a pick-ax, crowbar, shovel.
There will be nothing to dig
our way out of. The bodies
of anything still living will slip
silently through our own, heat
reaching our feet, moving into
our centers from the core of the earth.

DETOUR

We'd been expecting snow, but the sky
        had hardened and sunk. We locked
          the dove's cage.

When the rains came,
we tried to solve the riddle with books.

      Boxes of photographs were aging
on our shelves. In the dark,
        we couldn't distinguish

who was who, or even who
      was living. We heard a baby cry,

though we knew
      it didn't exist. Among the images of faces
        and landscapes we'd known

was a list of all of the beasts
we'd run over along the way.

      You read: raccoon, opossum,
family of skunks…We felt so close
      to an answer.

I was burning up inside.
      Your mouth had caught fire.

IF DECEMBER

If all the cages have keys, the throats
        of birds pinned to the wall.

The truck idles for days
        at the curb in front of the house.

The painted face of a dancer
        vanishes from a window. If the cup

holds. A slow leak, a full tub.
        If the saucer is flying

across the room, unexplained.
        If December

wakes in a white room
        without windows.

If we cannot keep its eyes
        clean by tearing phlox

from its roots. If not the dirt,
        the sun, the snow, the floods

will open us. If blood carries
        stories of creatures walking

with wings. Then the bleeding
        tongue, then the whipped

horse, then the muzzle.

ITCH

The nag tail-whipped flies from her back,
boys jumped from boats into rushes
to avoid being bitten. Even cranes left eggs

to hatch untended off marshy, wooded trails. So,
when our swatter's waffle-holes jellied yellow and red,

it was impossible to know whose blood it was.

The man lying on shore watched the boys
splash, disappear, while filling his mouth with flies,
then spiders, sparrows, like the old woman

who'd swallow anything living
to get rid of the tickle inside her.

But this has nothing to do with gain

or the soul's weight: it's about heat—
The train carries a woman in a winter coat,
carrying dirty bags full of dirty bags and empty bottles.

This is silently about the flies pouring from a slit
along the seam of her coat as she stands,

whispering: *this is my blood, this*

is my cup, and the secret way
I inch a pen down the back of my throat
to scratch out the ink of their crawling.

CHATEAUBRIAND

Love me here, a tangle in the wire, complicate
my limbs with your mouth. Like the trail,
we're a handful of breadcrumbs, the boy
whispering himself to sleep at the library,
the book slipping from his lap. We haven't
lived long enough to knot cherry stems

together with our tongues. A girl
from another town was pinned against a fence
with the grill of a pickup while jogging.
The guy behind the wheel, a stranger, lived
on her street. You see, it happens

like this: one day, you're eating Chateaubriand,
the next, you can barely pronounce *tender*,
or make use of the skin that preserved it…

…Tickle my feet as gravel once did.
Remind me of balms and salves to keep
our organs safe. Like a grape, leave me
in my skin, as I nestle in your cheek,
making a home of your darkest, inside spaces.

WHEN WE WERE PREY TO NOTHING

The doe hides her fawn in sedge
   and disappears in the corn.

Some days
     it's clear enough for love
   to depend on the periphery.

I sit in a willow between the field
   and marsh, doubt the red currant

and cattails, the farmer's
     rusted pickup and morgue
   of tires. All of it a milkdream

of a baby hidden in a car seat
   of a Corolla left in the parking lot

of Tan World, waiting
     for her mother...
   I'd be lying if I said

I didn't want to build
     a nest in these branches

to hide you.
     But when we were prey to nothing,
   we left fields and orchards untended—

they withered as we slept
   in full sun. And so it is:

you'll grow into your skin
                  through the flesh of fruit
           picked and eaten from every tree.

BUT I TO YOU OF A WHITE GOAT

a white squirrel, a birch tree. you of lips,
of snow adrift in streetlights. all the pasts
that recreate a lifetime but you

*

whispered. stark, the maple limbs quivered
as if to say, too, of white: it's spectral,
the way your finger hushes my lips

*

and you to me of a dull ax. all the lifetimes
that recreate a past. the tall grasses and ditches,
wheels collected to collapse

*

being unbodied, come, settle
between your high and low, your lap,
a manic love to fold my wasted bones upon

*

find nothing. there are whistles so pitched
to be white. an open mouth in winter,
a goat is, as I to you, the air

SPLENDOR

The worm writhing, tying its body into knots
in the grass, the body tearing in half, the millipedes

approaching. The millipedes taking over the living
body of the worm, my sister, who rinses the worm with water,

unraveling the body as I watch. The millipedes still searching
for their meal when I smear their bodies through the dirt

with my shoe. I am disgusted and enthralled and
in love. The baby grows too big for my womb. The flies

are small enough to slip through the screen toward the light
above the sink and fall into water around the faucet.

The spider's full belly. Its web in the window above the sink.
The other spiders who nest on the ceiling, and my husband,

who kills them on my behalf. The heaviness of the spider
as it scrambles to the last dry edge of toilet paper

before the water pulls it under. The oats that once grew
in a wet field that now rest in our bowls. My son

in his fourteenth year, my daughter almost in her first. The difference
between the moment of being and a moment of being.

When there's a body and when there is none.

IN THE BEGINNING

The names we create for the people we build
of sticks and mud and snow. The houses we fashion
for them to live in. The weather they must survive. All of it
slipping. The baby we implant in the dirt-womb
of a stick woman. The fetus slipping. The huts we build
on riverbeds, the mud pies we force into babies' mouths.
The tongue slipping. Lullabies in which we swaddle them,
rocking boughs in the wind and the breaking. Breaking. We must
build a shelter. Collect scrap and wood, blankets to save the bodies.
Imagine trees, cut the limbs, rebuild the bridges. Trust the sun
to hold us and not shine too keenly. To keep still as we gather
buckets of water, the surface rippling with heat. We will feed it
to the people. We will wash ourselves in light.

ACKNOWLEDGMENTS

Many thanks to the editors of the following journals, where poems from this collection originally appeared:

Aquifer: The Florida Review Online: "Reflex"
Arkansas International: "Confessional" and "Controlled Burn"
Baltimore Review: "On Earth as It Is in Heaven"
Barnstorm: "Krakow" and "Dear Abby"
Best New Poets 2013: "Preserving"
Bramble: "Rabbit in the Road"
Cimarron Review: "Itch"
Eleven Eleven: "A Drain Full of Eels"
Fugue: "And Still with Light in Your Eyes"
The Harlequin: "Home (iv)" and "Growing Season"
Hayden's Ferry Review: "Retrospective," "Muss Es Sein? Es Muss Sein!"
The Journal: "Self-Portrait as a Cat Trapped in a Hotel Room"
Kenyon Review Online: "Nothing to Undo That Can't Be Done Again," "Chateaubriand"
Linebreak: "Unfurling"
Memorious: "In the Beginning," "On the Eve of the Death of the Patron Saint of Those Whose Lives are Lost to Something Science Can't Explain"
Midwestern Gothic: "Painting the Garage," "Bake Sales"
New Poetry from the Midwest (New American Press): "Itch"
Poetry Northwest: "Splendor"
Poets on Growth (Math Paper Press): "Krakow," "Itch," "Unfurling," "Bake Sales, Anyway," "Preserving"
Post Road: "Wait in the Bathtub and It Will Carry You," "In Which I Hoard the Air Escaping"
Salamander: "Abandoned Nest"
Sugar House Review: "On My Way Home"
Sycamore Review: "All-Inclusive Trip to the Land of Milk & Honey"
The Adroit Journal: "When We Were Prey to Nothing," "Maps of Places Drawn to Scale"

Tinderbox: "Camouflage"
Verse Wisconsin: "At the Periphery, Where Life Hums"
Vinyl Poetry: "but I to you of a white goat," "Encourage Birds," "If
  December"

I'm indebted to the tremendous poets who've helped this book take shape
and breathe: Cynthia Marie Hoffmann, Rita Mae Reese, Jesse Lee Kercheval,
Nancy Reddy, Rebecca Dunham, Angela Sorby, and Danielle Jones (my PFF).
I am inspired by your words and appreciate your generous attention to mine.

My heartfelt gratitude to the teachers who encouraged and guided me along
the way: Lloyd Schwartz, Joyce Peseroff, Jill McDonough, Amaud Jamaul
Johnson, Quan Barry, Ronald Wallace, and Darren Defrain. Thanks to the
generous support of Sustainable Arts Foundation and Writers' Room of Bos-
ton for the gifts of time and space to write. Thank you to Traci Brimhall,
for selecting this book, and to Pleiades Press, especially Jenny Molberg, for
bringing it to life.

With love to my parents, Ellen Voras and John Voras, who read me nursery
rhymes and let me run through the fields and forests of Wisconsin, where
these poems took root. Thanks to Lisa and Joe Hills, who have supported
my writing in innumerable ways. To my family and friends who show up at
readings, answer my ridiculous questions, and watch my kids so I can write—
thanks for being my village. Phoebe and Felix, you keep my eyes open to the
beauty and terror of this world with the greatest intensity, and I am so grateful.

For Carter, who grew into a remarkable person while I wrote this book. And
for Matthew, with unspeakable gratitude and love.

ABOUT THE AUTHOR

ANGELA VORAS-HILLS grew up in Wisconsin and earned her MFA at University of Massachusetts-Boston. Her poems have appeared in *Kenyon Review Online*, *Best New Poets*, *Hayden's Ferry Review*, *Memorious*, and *New Ohio Review*, among other journals and anthologies. She has received grants from The Sustainable Arts Foundation and Key West Literary Seminar, as well as a fellowship at Writers' Room of Boston. She lives with her family in Milwaukee, WI.

THE LENA-MILES WEVER TODD PRIZE

The editors at Pleiades Press select 10-15 finalists from among those manuscripts submitted each year. An external judge selects one winner for publication. This year's judge was Traci Brimhall. All selections are made blind to authorship in and open competition for which any poet writing in English is eligible. Lena-Miles Wever Todd Prize for Poetry books are distributed by Louisiana State University Press.

ABOUT LENA-MILES WEVER TODD

Lena-Miles Wever Todd (1910-2000), for whom this prize is named, was a 1931 graduate of Winthrop College, where she was a Marshal and editor of *The Johnsonian*, the college newspaper. She was a lifelong poet, whose work was anthologized and privately published. She lived most of her life in Greenville, South Carolina, where she and her husband, Leonard M. Todd, supported and led numerous cultural organizations. She was also a painter. Her paintings are now in the collection of the Greenville County Museum of Art. Her family and friends created this prize in her honor.

ALSO AVAILABLE FROM PLEIADES PRESS

The Imaginary Age by Leanna Petronella
dark // thing by Ashley M. Jones
Destruction of the Lover by Luis Panini, translated by Lawrence Schimel
How to Tell If You Are Human: Diagram Poems by Jessy Randall
Fluid States by Heidi Czerwiec